THE PERSONALITY POTION

ALAN MacDONALD

Illustrated by John Eastwood

PACIFIC
LEARNING

© 2001 Pacific Learning
© 1996 Written by **Alan MacDonald**
Illustrated by **John Eastwood**
US Edit by **Alison Auch**

This Americanized Edition of *The Personality Potion*,
originally published in English in 1996, is published
by arrangement with Oxford University Press.

05 04 03 02 01
10 9 8 7 6 5 4 3 2 1

Published by
Pacific Learning
P.O. Box 2723
Huntington Beach, CA 92647-0723
www.pacificlearning.com

ISBN: 1-59055-034-X
PL-7405

Contents

Kit Kane, Kid Detective

Martin Doolan was doing what he liked best. He was curled up in his bed, reading a book.

He had a candy bar he'd been saving all day. (Candy bars were his second favorite thing.) The bedroom light was off. He was using a flashlight under the covers to read his new library book. It was called *Kit Kane, Kid Detective.*

Kit was on the trail of a gangster, Slugs Malloy. Slugs had kidnapped Kit's girlfriend, Susie, and taken her to a potato factory. He was about to put her in the peeler.

Unless Kit got there soon it would be too late. Susie would be served up as a plate of french fries.

Suddenly, the door burst open!

"Martin...? Where are you? What are you doing?"

It was Martin's mom. She turned on the light.

Martin stuck his head out. He blinked several times like a mole coming out of its hole.

"Nothing. I'm just reading."

"Martin, it's only six thirty. It's not anywhere near your bedtime."

"I know that, but I just want to read my book."

"Why don't you do something fun? Call one of your friends."

"I don't want to. I'm busy."

"Why don't you go over to the park? Go and play basketball or something."

"Oh, Mom! I'd rather just stay here and read."

His mom gave him one of her looks. The look that meant he should be out doing things. His parents were always saying stuff like this.

"Don't you want to play with your friends?" Or, "You really need to get out more."

Martin couldn't help it. He didn't want to go play basketball at the park. He'd rather watch TV or read a book, especially if the book was as good as the Kit Kane detective series.

His mom said, "You know you can't spend your life hiding in your room." She sighed heavily and shut the door.

Martin got up and turned off the light. In the dark, he pretended he was Kit Kane sneaking into the factory to save Susie. He crawled on his hands and knees toward the bed.

"Okay, Slugs, this is the end of the line for you!" he said in his best gangster voice.

He dived on his pillow and wrestled it to the floor. In the fight that followed, his candy bar took a little damage – but it was all in the line of duty.

The Empty Seat

The next day got off to a bad start.
The school bus was crowded. His best
friend, Sparrow, waved to him, but the
seat next to him was taken. The only
empty seat was next to the dreaded
Duncan Lomax.

Lomax was a year ahead, and Martin
always kept out of his way. He'd seen
Lomax pick on younger kids in the
playground. He made them give him
their lunches.

If they argued, Lomax followed
them around until they were too
scared not to give up their lunches.

Martin pretended he hadn't seen the empty seat, but Lomax had seen him.

"There's a seat here, Four Eyes. I'm not going to eat you."

Martin sat down. He hated being called Four Eyes.

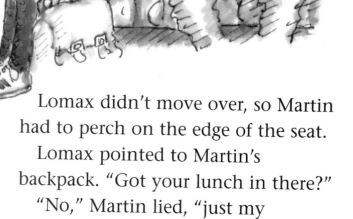

Lomax didn't move over, so Martin had to perch on the edge of the seat.

Lomax pointed to Martin's backpack. "Got your lunch in there?"

"No," Martin lied, "just my homework."

Lomax nodded. He pretended to be looking out of the window. Then he grabbed for Martin's bag.

Martin held on, but Lomax was stronger. Martin's arm hurt from trying to hang on to his backpack.

"Let's see what's *really* in here," said Lomax, unzipping the backpack.

He took out Martin's lunchbox and said in a dumb voice, "Look at this – sandwiches! Your mom must have sneaked your lunch in here."

Everyone on the bus was looking at them now. Martin saw Laura Alvarez watching. Laura was in his grade. With her thick black hair and dark eyes she was just the kind of girl Kit Kane would have as his girlfriend.

Lomax was sniffing Martin's cheese sandwiches. He turned up his nose and went to put them back. Then he saw the candy bar at the bottom of the lunchbox.

"This will do just fine. Thanks, Four Eyes," he said, pulling off the wrapper.

"That's mine! Give it back," Martin said hopelessly.

Lomax grinned and took a big bite. "Mmm, not bad, Four Eyes. You better have another one of these for me next time I ask you."

Martin turned away.

In his imagination, he pictured what would happen next if he were Kit Kane.

Kit stood up and pulled Lomax out of his seat by his jacket.

"Why doncha pick on someone your own size, dogbreath?" he drawled.

"D-don't hurt me," stammered Lomax.

*Kit swung Lomax around his head
three times and let go. Lomax flew
through the air and landed in the lap
of a surprised old lady who thumped him
with her umbrella. The whole bus cheered.*

Unfortunately, that only happened
in Martin's imagination. In reality, he
sat there staring out of the window.

He knew his face was red. He felt stupid and helpless.

Sparrow ran after him as they went into school. He was the smallest boy in their class and always seemed to be running to keep up.

"Hi, Marty. I saw what Lomax did to you on the bus," he chirped.

"Thanks for reminding me."

"He's just a big oaf."

"Yeah," Martin muttered.

"I bet if anyone had the guts to stand up to him, he'd cry like a baby."

Martin stopped suddenly. "I didn't see you doing anything to help."

Sparrow looked surprised. "What could I do? I was only saying..."

"Yeah, well, don't say it – unless you're going to do something. That's the trouble around here. No one ever does anything."

Sparrow went away to hang up his coat. He looked hurt. Martin didn't know why he'd said that. He just felt angry inside. Angry with Lomax. Angry with himself for looking stupid in front of everyone else.

Martin's teacher, Ms. Schwartz, had some news for them. Anyone who wanted a part in the new school play should come to the audition next Monday.

Martin wasn't usually interested in the school plays. Once, in first grade, he'd been a sheep in a play. All he had to do was say "Baa!" then lie down and go to sleep.

This year, though, the play was *Bugsy Malone*. It had music and songs, and, best of all, it was about old-time gangsters. Martin was spellbound as Ms. Schwartz told them the story.

He began to imagine himself playing the part of Bugsy. He'd borrow his dad's old suit and wear a hat pulled down over one eye. He'd chew gum and talk in his Kit Kane accent.

By the time Ms. Schwartz had finished talking, Martin knew he'd be perfect for the part of Bugsy.

It was a great idea, but it wouldn't work. Mainly he knew he didn't have the nerve to try for the part. The thought of standing up in front of everyone made him feel sick inside.

The Potion

On the way home from school, Martin stopped at his Uncle Hal's. Uncle Hal was an inventor. The trouble was, Uncle Hal never finished any of his inventions. He always said they still needed "a little fine-tuning."

Then he forgot all about them and started on something else. Martin had really liked the battery-powered straw that made milk bubble by itself.

The underwater chess set had been another good idea, but Uncle Hal couldn't remember where he'd put it. His garage was crammed to the ceiling with old pipes, tubes, boxes, bottles, and wires. He spent most of his time looking for things.

Martin banged three times on the garage door. It lifted up and there was Uncle Hal, wearing a pair of purple glasses. The glasses had two small lightbulbs on the top of the frames. Uncle Hal touched a button behind his ear. The glasses lit up.

"Pretty clever, aren't they? What do you think?" he asked.

"They're amazing," said Martin. "What are they for?"

"Seeing in the dark." Uncle Hal shut the garage door behind them. He turned off the lamp on his workbench.

"Now, imagine there's a power outage, and you don't have a flashlight. You turn on your Glow Glasses and – presto! – you can see."

"Can I try them?" asked Martin, taking off his own glasses.

Martin turned on the Glow Glasses.
"All I can see are two blobs of light.
They hurt my eyes," he said,
disappointed.

"I know," said Uncle Hal. "They still
need a little fine-tuning."

He turned the lamp back on and
started to take his invention apart.

"So, how was school today?"

"Terrible," said Martin.

"Usual terrible, or something new?"

"There's this kid named Lomax. He picked on me on the bus today. He's about ten times my size. He grabbed my backpack and stole my candy bar."

"He sounds like a regular crook."

"Yep. And you know what I did? With the whole bus watching, I sat there like an idiot and did nothing."

"I'd say that is sensible. Never take on a bully ten times your size for the sake of a candy bar. After all, when did a candy bar ever fight for you?"

Martin shrugged. "That wasn't the worst thing. They're going to do this play at school. It's called *Bugsy Malone,* and it's about old-time gangsters."

Uncle Hal raised one eyebrow. "So what's so bad about this play?"

"Nothing, it's great. I'd like to be in it. I really want to be Bugsy, but I can't."

"Why not?"

"I won't be able to make it through the audition. I'll be so nervous I'll open my mouth and nothing will come out. No one's going to pick me to play Bugsy Malone."

Uncle Hal looked at Martin.

"You really don't think you can get the part?"

Martin sadly shook his head.

"Well, come and see me on Sunday. It'll take some work, but I might be able to help."

Uncle Hal wouldn't say anything else. He just tapped his nose and said, "Sunday."

Martin thought about it all week. What could Uncle Hal do to help him get the part of Bugsy Malone?

Early on Sunday morning he rang Uncle Hal's doorbell. Uncle Hal led Martin into the garage.

"Ready?" he asked. Martin nodded. He didn't have any idea what was going to happen.

Uncle Hal picked up two test tubes. In one was some inky-green liquid. In the other was some white powder.

He carefully poured a little from each test tube into a bottle.

"What is it?" whispered Martin.

"Something I've been working on all week. I call it my Personality Potion."

"Personality Potion?" Martin's eyes widened. "What's that?"

"It brings out all the hidden talents that no one knows are inside you. You'll see."

Uncle Hal mixed the potion in the bottle. It foamed and fizzed.

He held it up to the lamp. The potion seemed to glow in the light as if it were full of stars. Martin took the bottle and looked at it in wonder.

"You mean this can help me get the part in the play?"

"You'll be magnificent."

"How do you know it really works?"

"See for yourself. Try it tomorrow," said Uncle Hal.

He opened the garage door. Martin went out into the bright morning light, holding the Personality Potion tight in his hand.

Do I Seem Different?

When he woke up Monday morning, Martin thought the potion must have been a dream. Yet there it was, still on his bedside table.

He took off the lid and sniffed it. Then he took a small sip. The taste was sweet and bitter at the same time. Martin drank some more and let it slip down his throat.

Jumping out of bed, he ran to look in the bathroom mirror.

There was no doubt something had happened to him. His head didn't droop and his eyes were brighter than usual. He didn't even feel worried about the day ahead at school.

Martin sat next to Sparrow on the bus. He could see Duncan Lomax in the back. He hoped that Lomax had forgotten about the candy bar. Martin had one in his backpack, but he didn't want to give it up.

Sparrow was talking about some science-fiction movie he'd seen on TV, but Martin found it hard to listen. He was wondering whether he looked different to anyone. The Personality Potion was in his pocket – just in case he needed more.

He looked over at Laura Alvarez. Could she see any change in him?

"Do I seem different to you?" he asked Sparrow suddenly.

Sparrow blinked at him. "I was telling you about the part with the aliens in it."

"I know, I just wondered if I seem any different."

Sparrow looked closely. "Nope. You've got green skin and three heads, as usual."

At recess, Martin and Sparrow talked about the school play. Sparrow said Mark Shaw would probably get the part of Bugsy. Mark was the class athlete, and he got picked for everything. Martin said he might even try out for the part himself.

Sparrow gasped. "You? You want to play Bugsy Malone?"

Before Martin could answer, he saw Lomax. He was on the other side of the playground and was coming straight toward them.

Martin didn't have any time to think. Quickly, he fumbled for the Personality Potion and took a swallow. If it really worked, he desperately needed it now.

A group of girls stood between Lomax and Martin. Lomax barged right through the middle, and one girl fell while trying to get out of his way. Martin had just noticed that it was Laura Alvarez when Lomax reached them.

"Four Eyes! Where have you been?"

"Oh, I've been around. Why?"

"Where's my candy bar? I told you to bring me one."

"He must have forgotten," Sparrow said bravely.

"Who asked you, Peewee?" Lomax said, glaring at him.

Lomax held out his hand to Martin. "One candy bar, Four Eyes. You'd better hand it over."

"It's in my backpack," said Martin, "but there's one problem."

"Oh yeah, what?"

"You can't have it."

He was amazed at the words he'd just spoken. It must have been the potion! Lomax's mouth was open but nothing was coming out.

"Say that again," he said at last.

"I said it's my candy bar. You can get lost."

A crowd was gathering around them. Martin could see Laura and her friends at the front. No one had ever told Lomax to get lost before, and they wanted to see what would happen.

Martin felt scared and brave all at the same time. It was as if the potion had popped a cork inside him.

Lomax grabbed Martin's arm and shook it – as if he were four years old.

"Where's my candy bar?! Go get it!"

"No," Martin said coolly. "You should lay off the candy, Lomax. Your teeth and gums are turning green."

"What did you say?" Lomax howled.

"They're green. Everyone calls you Gross Gums."

The kids laughed. They couldn't believe their ears. Here was quiet Martin Doolan, standing up to the worst bully in school!

Lomax was furious. He shook Martin's arm again.

Then he heard Laura Alvarez shout, "Let him go, Gross Gums!" Someone else repeated it, and soon the whole crowd was chanting:

"Gross Gums! Gross Gums!"

Lomax stared at them, his face as red as ketchup. He liked to pick on younger kids when they were alone. He wasn't used to facing a whole crowd shouting at him.

The noise had reached a teacher who was heading toward the group.

Lomax let go of Martin and ran off.

Martin watched him go. It was
incredible! He had stood up to Lomax
and survived. The potion had really
worked. It changed him into a
different person – someone who could
do or say anything.

People were staring at him in a new
way. One of them was Laura.

"Thanks for starting that," he said
to her.

Laura smiled. "Serves him right. Is your arm okay?"

"Yeah. He was only holding it for show," Martin said bravely.

"What got into you?" asked Laura. "He's a whole lot bigger than you are, you know."

"I was sick of him. I had to do something."

Just then, the bell rang. "Well, see you later," said Laura. "Are you going to the audition this afternoon?"

"Yes... yes, I am," said Martin hastily. "I'm trying out for the part of Bugsy."

He walked away feeling six feet tall. He'd talked to Laura Alvarez. After a whole year, he'd finally talked to her, and she hadn't laughed at him. She'd talked back. Then he remembered: he'd said he was going to the audition.

Even worse, he'd said he was trying out for the lead role. The part of Bugsy. How could his mouth have landed him in so much trouble?

The Big Scene

Martin sat in one of the chairs in the auditorium, waiting for his turn to audition. A lot of people had come to watch. They filled four rows of chairs. Laura Alvarez sat with her friend, Yasmin. Mark Shaw was there with his usual friends.

Martin sat by himself. Sparrow hadn't come because he said he couldn't stand to see Martin make a fool of himself.

It was almost Martin's turn. He clutched the potion nervously. The bottle felt hot and sticky. As long as he could drink it just before he got on stage, everything would be okay.

The last person before Martin was Lomax, who thought he was perfect for the role of an old-time gangster. Ms. Schwartz gave him a page of *Bugsy* to read.

Lomax was the world's worst actor. He read the lines as if they were the weather report. There were a few sniggers from the back rows. Lomax looked up furiously.

"Thank you, Duncan," said Ms. Schwartz. "Martin, you're next."

Martin took a deep breath and stood up. He heard Mark Shaw whisper to his friends, "Martin Doolan? This should be hilarious."

Martin unscrewed the lid of the potion and got up to walk to the stage. As he got to the end of the row, he lifted the bottle to take a drink. Lomax, on his way back to his seat, barged into him on purpose.

"Oh, sorry, Four Eyes, I didn't see you there!"

The bottle spun out of Martin's hand and smashed all over the floor.

Martin looked down in horror at the green puddle by his feet.

"Come on, Martin, you'll have to clean that up later," called Ms. Schwartz, in her annoyed voice.

Martin stood in front of everyone while she scolded him for bringing drinks into the auditorium. Then she pointed to the page. "Now, start there and read to the bottom."

Martin tried to think about the words, but they seemed to swim around like tadpoles on the page. Without the Personality Potion, he knew he couldn't do it. He couldn't even speak. His throat was dry and his face was burning up.

He made a sound like a car engine trying to start.

"Uhhrrr!"

Looking up, he could see Mark Shaw and his friends cracking up.

"Speak up, Four Eyes, we can't hear you!" yelled Lomax from the back of the auditorium.

Martin's gaze shifted to Laura
Alvarez. She was glaring at Lomax.
Then she looked straight at Martin and
nodded. "Come on!" she mouthed.

Martin was amazed. Why would she
care that he was making a complete
fool of himself? He shut his eyes. He
tried to think how Kit Kane would
have read the part. Then he took a
deep breath and started to read.

After a while he realized that the laughing had stopped. The auditorium was quiet. Everyone was listening. He was doing it! He was saying the lines in the voice he'd practiced hundreds of times under his blankets.

The longer he went on, the better it sounded.

"Well done, Martin!" said Ms. Schwartz when he'd finished. "I had no idea you were hiding all this talent." She sounded very impressed.

Martin walked off the stage in a daze to clean up the broken glass.

As he was sweeping up what was left of the potion bottle, Laura Alvarez was called to the stage. Martin was surprised to see how nervous she looked. He gave her his friendliest smile as she passed him.

"Go for it," he whispered. "It's easy once you get started."

The Truth

A few days later, Martin stopped outside Uncle Hal's garage. He banged three times on the door. It lifted up and a hand pulled him inside.

"Martin! You're just in time!"

"I can't see, Uncle Hal. Turn the light on."

Instead, Uncle Hal took off Martin's glasses and replaced them with another pair. There was a click and two small beams of light lit up the room.

"The Glow Glasses! You finished them!" said Martin.

"That's right, Martin. They just needed a little fine-tuning," Uncle Hal said proudly.

"You're a genius, Uncle Hal. That Personality Potion was amazing."

Uncle Hal looked blank for a moment. Then his face lit up.

"You mean it worked? You got the part in the play?"

"You're looking at Bugsy Malone," said Martin. "You should have seen Mark Shaw's face when Ms. Schwartz told everyone."

Martin went on to tell Uncle Hal the whole story of what had happened with Lomax and the audition. Laura had gotten a part as a singer, so he'd be seeing her all the time.

"It was funny, though," he said finally. "I auditioned without drinking the potion. I guess I must have still been feeling the effects."

He looked at Uncle Hal, who was grinning from ear to ear.

"What? What's so funny?"

"Would you like to see what was in that Personality Potion?" said Uncle Hal. He went into the kitchen and came back with two bottles. One contained the green liquid and the other, white powder. He showed Martin the labels.

"Green food coloring and baking soda. That gave it the fizz," said Uncle Hal. "Your aunt and I use them for our baking. That's all I put in the potion."

Martin stared at the bottles in disbelief. "You mean it was all a trick? There wasn't really a Personality Potion, Uncle Hal?"

Uncle Hal shook his head, still grinning.

"Then how did it change me?" asked Martin. "I was a different person."

"It worked because you believed in the potion, but really, you were just believing in yourself. There was no magic at all."

"Wow!" said Martin. He didn't know whether to be mad or happy.

He'd wanted to ask Uncle Hal for more of the Personality Potion, but it turned out that he didn't need it. From now on he'd just have to get by on his own.

"I guess when you think about it, I must actually be pretty normal," he said out loud.

"Normal? Who wants to be normal?" said Uncle Hal, putting on his purple Glow Glasses. "I'd say anyone who got the lead role in the school play must be pretty special."

About the Author

I have been writing stories
for radio, television, and
books for many years.
I live in England and work
in an attic room where
no one can disturb me.

I sometimes try out
my stories on my two
children at bath time. If they stop shouting
and splashing me, I know that it must be a
good story.

This story was inspired by reading
Dr. Jekyll and Mr. Hyde, by Robert Louis
Stevenson. I started thinking about what
would happen if a boy had a potion that
gave him "extra" personality – instead of
turning him into a monster.

Alan MacDonald